JUICE

POWER

Teoorah B. N. Shaleahk

Book Publishing Company
Summertown, TN

© 2005 Teoorah B. N. Shaleahk

Cover design: Warren Jefferson
Interior design: Gwynelle Dismukes
Photography: Warren Jefferson

Published in the United States by
Book Publishing Company
P.O. Box 99
Summertown, TN 38483
1-888-260-8458

Pictured on the cover:
Fresh Quench, p. 29
Vegetable Combo
  One, pp. 22–23

Printed in the United States

ISBN 1-57067-168-0

10 09 08 07 06 05   6 5 4 3 2 1

Shaleahk, Teoorah B. N.
Juice power / by Teoorah B. N. Shaleahk
       p. cm.
  Includes index.
  ISBN 1-57067-168-0
  1. Beverages. 2. Fruit juices. 3. Vegetable juices. 4. Self-care, Health.
  I. Title.

  TX815.S53 2005
  641.8'75—dc22

                                          2005027648

CONTENTS

Introduction 7–18

Nutritional Recommendations, Sweeteners, Hints for Making Great-Tasting Juices, Food Combining, Blenders and Other Equipment, Abbreviations and Equivalents

Lose Weight 19

Watermelon Juice 20–21
Vegetable Combo One 22–23
Purification 24

Cleanse Your System 25

Detoxification 26
Daily Grape Drink 27

Strengthen Your Immune System 28

Fresh Quench 29
Ginger Get Well 30
Vegetable Combo Two 31

Increase Your Energy Level 32

Everlasting Life 33
Quick-Me-Up 34
The Resurrection 35
Vegetable Combo Three 36

Elevate Your Mood 37

Pick-Me-Up Coconut Date Shake 38
Fruity Ice Cream Soy Shake 39
Mango Melody 40
Vegetable Combo Four 41

Increase Your Stamina 42

Last Man (or Woman) Standing 43
Pineapple Supreme Piña Colada 44
Vegetable Combo Five 45

Memory, Clarity, and Focus 46

Peach Deliverance 47
Second Resurrection 48
Cucumber Lemonade 49
Vegetable Combo Six 50

Relax Your Nerves 51

Eternity Winter 52
Hebrew Sunrise 53

Balance Your Being 54

Lemonade 55
Tropical Cooler 56

Protein Power 57

Hazelnut Heaven 58
Protein Shake for Strong Nails, Hair, and Skin 59
Vegetable Combo Seven 60

Revive Your System 61

Cranberry Crunch 62–63
Rehydration Drink 64
Very Berry Fine 65
Vegetable Combo Eight 66

Master Your Mornings! 67

Banana Breeze 68
Oat Breakfast Shake 69

Make Your Children Smile 70

Fresh Freeze 71
Kiwi Lemonade 72

Increase Body Mass 73

Tropical Dream 74
Banana Moon 75

Fruit Salads, Pie, and Pudding 76

Tropical Trees Fruit Salad with Fruit Sauce 77
Mango Banana Fruit Salad with Fruit Sauce 78–79
Georgia Peach Treat Fruit Salad with Fruit Sauce 80–81
Fruitropica Salad with Fruit Sauce 82
Mango-Papaya Pudding 83
Fruit "Un-Pie" 84

Glossary 85–91

Index 92–95

A SPECIAL NOTE OF THANKS

In regard to all those who have contributed to this work, no efforts have gone unnoticed. Special appreciation goes to all those who have helped edit this work in its initial stages.

Abba Gadol, thank you for every "i" that you dotted and every "t" you crossed! I am forever humbled. Yafah Asiel, Sevolet E. Aylohn, Rofah (Doctor) Afrah, thank you for allowing me to sit at your feet! You are truly an amazing wealth of wisdom...I love you!.

To the two phenomenal women who guide and help me always... E. Yoninah, thanks for the support! E. Elidah, there are no words great enough to encompass the love, comfort, and support you give to me!

To my mother Geneva, may we work together to bring the health and wellness you deserve into your life. It is attainable!

To A. Yatsiliel and Attorney Jacalyn Scott, all of your time and energy are priceless!

To all those who encouraged me throughout this process, N. Rahm, Marjorie Simon Esq., Tahmah, Dione Spears N.D... you are truly four irreplaceable people!

And last but not certainly not least, Prince Asiel, for your unlimited vision, your continuous guidance, endless support, and vast insight! Your perspicacious qualities are as immense as the Red Sea! You are such an inspiration. I am forever thankful for your friendship! This work was inspired by the great love you have for the health of all people!

Sincerely,
Teoorah B. N Shaleahk

INTRODUCTION

In just the past few decades, people as a whole have become sicker, more depressed, more obese, and more dependent on medications and prescription drugs than at any other time in history. How has this happened? Food manufacturers, marketing firms, and even health professionals have misled us about food, fitness, and well-being. Mistaken beliefs and urban legends have become so pervasive and widely accepted that when people hear, "Eat right!" they generally think Slim Fast, Jenny Craig, and Weight Watchers. Could the mind-set that brought us to such imbalance and ill health possibly set us free? Perhaps it is time to develop a new way of thinking—one that will restore our bodies and minds to their natural state of vitality, strength, stamina, and wholeness.

This book offers a road map to that new mind-set. Depending on your current physical condition, dietary awareness, and eating habits, the guidance presented here can assist you in getting on the path to optimum health and help keep you there.

Although I am only in my early twenties, I have made many foolish choices in my life regarding my health. I am very glad that someone cared enough to intervene and show me a new direction, and I am also very thankful that I was open to hearing and following the advice I was given.

The care and kindness I was granted motivated me to be a part of a phenomenal business, Soul Vegetarian Restaurants, where I could offer the benefits of good health to others. I now am one of the owners of a full-service, all-natural juice bar where we serve delicious, dairy-free ice cream, make fresh juice drinks, and sell a variety of teas, natural cosmetics, and personal care products. And did I mention that in the restaurants we also serve amazing, fresh-baked vegan cakes, cookies, cinnamon rolls, as well as a variety of salads and other great vegan foods?

I am involved in more than half a dozen such enterprises worldwide as part of Soul Vegetarian Restaurants. Through my work I've discovered a growing interest in good health, and that interest is starting to spread. People all over the world are beginning to take their well-being more seriously and are willing to dedicate themselves to learning more about natural healing, regeneration, and living well. I've met countless people who were suffering from heartbreaking health conditions. It has been a blessing to assist them with becoming better informed about their health and to help them turn their distressing situations into success stories.

Knowledge is like an unlit match. Only after we strike the match by applying knowledge to our lives can we find our way out of the darkness. I've been asked countless times to share the recipes for my healing juices, and so I offer them to you in faith that they will be a guiding light for your good health. I pray that as you shift from one paradigm to the next, you will take with you the following OATH OF RESPONSIBILITY:

> As I enter into the higher realms of consciousness concerning my health, I vow to invest in my personal well-being so that I may reap the dividends that come with investing wisely. I will refrain from using words like "try," "can't," or "maybe" when it comes to making the right choices for myself. I will share my knowledge with those I love and do my very best to assist them in finding the road to optimum health and healing.

DISCLAIMER

Awareness is the key to optimum health. When we live life in true awareness, we are better equipped to make wise choices. As a passenger on the road to optimum health, you will find many markers along the way. This book is one of those markers. The suggestions, information, and recipes presented here are not intended to replace any diagnosis or treatment by your physician, nutritionist, or health care provider.

Nutritional Recommendations

A SIMPLE NUTRITION GUIDE:

- Eat all the raw fruits and vegetables you wish—the more the better!

- If you are hungry between meals and feel that you need a quick snack, try eating fresh fruit or a few nuts. Dried, unsulfured fruit with no added sugar or preservatives makes a great snack.

- Nuts and seeds (such as sesame, sunflower, and pumpkin) and their butters (such as almond or cashew butter or sesame tahini) are wholesome, nutritious snacks.

- If you have a health problem, consult a physician who is trained in nutrition before you make any radical changes to your diet.

EAT HEALTHFULLY! AVOID THE 7 HAZARDS OF GOOD NUTRITION:

- Alcohol
- Artificial sweeteners
- Caffeine and caffeinated beverages
- Dairy products
- Meat
- Soda
- Sugar

BREAKFAST

To start your day and flush the toxins out of your body, drink 12–16 ounces of fresh water. Eat a variety of fruits and drink plenty of water (the more the better). Try at least one unfamiliar fruit each week. Here are just a few of the many fruits you can try: apples, apricots, bananas, blueberries, cherries, cranberries, grapefruit, grapes, kiwifruit, melons, oranges, peaches, pears, pineapple, plums, raspberries, star fruit, strawberries, and tangerines.

LUNCH AND DINNER

Some people feel that eating a meal comprised of 80 percent cooked foods and 20 percent raw foods helps them maintain a healthy balance. A sample meal based on this ratio might consist of a baked potato, string beans, breaded eggplant, and a large fresh spinach salad topped with carrots, olives, sprouts, cucumbers, and tomatoes.

Choose one of the following for lunch or dinner:

- Leafy green salad (use either finely chopped spinach or lettuce as a base) with lots of raw vegetables, such as red, green, and yellow bell peppers; cucumbers; carrots; sunflower sprouts; olives; and tomatoes. Top it with a delicious, healthful salad dressing.
- Fruit salad, using a variety of fruit.
- Fruit or vegetable drinks made with blended fruit or vegetables.
- Vegetable soup or stew.

Do your homework! Study nutrition books, read articles, visit your local natural food store, and talk with the people you meet while shopping. You may be surprised at the wealth of information you will find.

Sweeteners

Our modern culture, with its growing reliance on highly processed foods, has become dependent on refined sweeteners for a quick source of energy and to elevate sluggish moods (which usually are followed by the well-known "sugar crash"). Sugar is an ingredient in nearly every packaged food we buy, even though it may not be obvious. The ubiquitous use of sugar in everything from breakfast cereals to breads, soups, sauces, salad dressings, soft drinks, and, of course, desserts, has given us an insatiable sweet tooth. In addition to the sugar found in processed foods, we add it by the spoonful to our coffee and tea and even lavish it on otherwise healthful foods such as oatmeal and smoothies. While no type of sugar should be relied on as a source of nutrition, it is possible to satisfy our cravings with more natural and wholesome alternatives. Here are some good choices:

NATURAL SWEETENERS

Barley Malt: This thick, sticky, deep brown syrup is made from sprouted barley. Look for it at your natural food store.

Dates: Similar in appearance to a giant raisin, this fruit has a single, elongated seed in the center. Dates should always be pitted before slicing or blending. To soften hard dates, soak them in warm water. This very sweet fruit is rich in fiber and several minerals. Date sugar, which is made from pulverized dried dates, is available in natural food stores.

Fruit: Fresh fruit adds abundant natural sweetness to shakes and other sweet foods. Dried fruit has a more concentrated sweetness that both adults and children find appealing.

Honey: Honey is made by honeybees who combine plant nectar, a sweet substance secreted by flowers, with enzymes from their stomachs. Unfiltered, unheated, unprocessed "raw" honey offers the best quality and taste. Honey is very sticky and is usually packaged in a plastic or glass bottle. It is typically golden brown, although the color and sweetness of honey varies depending on the flower nectar it is made from.

Maple Syrup: Syrup is the most common form of maple sugar, although powdered and granulated maple sugar are also available. Grade B maple syrup is very sweet, thick, flavorful, and rich tasting (and is the one I most recommend). Pure maple syrup is typically packaged in plastic or glass bottles with the grade letter printed on the front. Grade B syrup is dark brown, depending on what region it comes from, while grade A syrup is usually lighter in both color and taste. Grade C is difficult to find, but is the most minerally rich.

Stevia: This sweet-tasting, highly concentrated, green plant extract is available as a powder or liquid. Stevia helps to regulate blood sugar and is often used by diabetics. A little goes a long way, so use it with care.

SWEETENERS TO AVOID

Artificial Sweeteners: Saccharin, aspartame, and other synthetic sweeteners offer virtually no nutritional benefit to our health or well-being. The word "artificial" says it all!

Dextrose: This sweetener is made from starch and is used to flavor many processed foods and beverages.

High-Fructose Corn Syrup: This is corn syrup that has been treated with enzymes to make it taste much sweeter than even refined sugar. It is found in many processed and packaged foods.

Refined Sugar: Excessive consumption of refined sugar, made from sugar cane or sugar beets, is believed to be associated with many common health problems: hypoglycemia, diabetes, heart disease, high cholesterol, obesity, indigestion, dermatitis, hyperactivity, lack of concentration, depression, anxiety, and more. Sugar also greatly increases the risk of dental decay. Refined sugar is an "empty food," devoid of vitamins, minerals, and fiber.

Hints for Making Healthy, Great-Tasting Shakes and Juices

- Always use the highest-quality, in-season fruits and vegetables.

- Use only natural ingredients. Treat your body like a temple, and invest in it as you would your home, car, education, or family.

- Whenever possible, use fresh (rather than canned or frozen) fruits and vegetables. Fresh fruits and vegetables contain active enzymes that are destroyed through cooking and canning. In addition, most store-bought frozen and canned foods contain preservatives, salt, sugar, or food coloring.

- Soak nuts and seeds in room temperature water overnight or for a minimum of 8–12 hours. Soaking makes nuts and seeds easier to digest, especially when they are eaten with other foods. In very hot temperatures or climates, place the soaking nuts and seeds in the refrigerator to prevent spoilage.

- Use carob instead of chocolate or cocoa. Carob is made from the roasted and ground seed pods of a tropical locust tree. This sweet, brown powder is rich in calcium and potassium. It contains none of the harmful substances found in chocolate, and therefore is neither mood altering nor addictive. Chocolate is made from the beans of the delicate cacao tree. It is a stimulant that is combined with refined sugar and usually dairy products to make candy bars and other confections. It is high in saturated fat and contains caffeine as well as a caffeine-like substance called theobromine. Chocolate is acid forming and can irritate the digestive system. Many people find chocolate to be habit forming; it also is a common trigger for migraine headaches.

- Stay clear of all dairy products; use dairy-free alternatives instead, such as soymilk, rice milk, and almond milk. Natural food stores carry a wide array of options, and even many supermarkets now have natural food sections where dairy alternatives are stocked.

- For the highest quality and freshest taste, drink your shakes and juices shortly after they are blended. After about fifteen minutes, the beverage may begin to separate and certain ingredients may lose some of their potency. If you must let your drink sit for a while (for instance, if you're making a shake in the morning to drink later in the day), reblend it or shake it vigorously in a sealed container. If you are able to reblend it, add a few small ice cubes to help cool the shake from the heat produced by the rotating blades of the blender.

- If you have an upset stomach or digestive problems, you might want to avoid combining fruits and vegetables at the same meal, especially foods from the cabbage family or melons, both of which can wreak havoc on an already sensitive system.

Food Combining

The sun provides light, heat, and energy, and aids in the process of photosynthesis. The earth provides shelter and the necessary nutrients for plants to grow. The ecology of life is dependent on the balance and interrelationship of all living things. This understanding can help us remember the basic guidelines of food combining. Simply put, some foods are more compatible than others. The right food combinations can improve digestion and the absorption of nutrients.

Many people find that following the "80:20 rule" (that is, a diet of 80 percent alkalizing foods and 20 percent acidifying foods) keeps them feeling balanced, energetic, healthy, and regular. While this rule works well in general, it is very important to listen to your body and pay attention to your individual needs. Observe how various combinations of foods affect your mood, sleep patterns, energy level, and hair, skin, eyes, and nails, and make adjustments accordingly.

Food Combining Grid

ACIDIFYING FOODS

Fruits:
blueberries
cherries
citrus (all, except lemons)
cranberries
kiwifruit
prunes

Other:
alcohol
animal products and by-products

caffeine and decaffeinated products
carob
chocolate
cocoa
coffee
dairy products (animal milk, cheese, yogurt, butter, ice cream, etc.)
eggs
fish
food coloring and dyes

meat
some multivitamin and mineral supplements
peanuts
pickles and pickled foods
poultry
preserved foods
sodas and soft drinks
sugar
tobacco
vinegar

ALKALIZING FOODS

Vegetables:
alfalfa sprouts
artichokes
asparagus
barley grass
basil
beets
bell peppers
broccoli
brussels sprouts
cabbage
carrots
cauliflower
celery
chard
collard greens
corn
cucumber
dandelions
edible flowers
eggplants
garlic
ginger
green peas
horseradish
jalapeño peppers
kale
lettuce
mushrooms
mustard greens
okra
onions
parsnips
peas
pumpkin
radish
rutabaga
scallions
spinach
sprouts
squash
turnip greens
watercress
yams

Sea Vegetables:
arame
blue-green algae
dulse
hijiki
kelp
kombu
nori
spirulina
wakame

Fruits:
apples
apricots
avocados
bananas
cantaloupe
cherries
currants
dates
figs
grapes
honeydew
lemons
melons
papaya
peaches
pears
tangerines
watermelon

Teas:
dandelion
herbal
ginger
ginseng
green

Other:
almonds
bee pollen
Brazil nuts
chestnuts
cinnamon
flaxseeds
hazelnuts
honey
lecithin
mineral water
royal jelly
sesame seeds
stevia
sunflower seeds
water

Blenders and Other Equipment

Blender: This electrical appliance uses short, rotating blades to chop, blend, purée, and liquefy foods.

Centrifugal Juicer: This electrical machine pulverizes foods by using a fixed, swift-spinning blade or sharp grated plate propelled by an outward blade that separates the pulp and juice by centrifugal force. This is the most common and affordable type of juicer used for juicing carrots and other hard vegetables, as well as softer vegetables and fruits.

Grater: Many food processors and blenders come with a grater attachment that is used to shred food into fine pieces. Manual graters come in flat, cylindrical, and box shapes, and are made of metal or plastic.

Grinder: This stand-alone electrical device or attachment to a food processor or blender reduces food into small particles of varying sizes. Manual grinders, operated by a hand crank, are available as well.

Reamer: This is a ridged, teardrop-shaped tool with a handle. It also is available as an attachment to a food processor or blender. Reamers are primarily used to juice citrus fruits.

Trituration and Filtered Pressing: During this process, food is pulverized by hard rubbing or grinding, then squeezed through a filtered hydraulic press. The equipment for this method can be quite costly.

> **Question:** What is the best blender?
>
> **Answer:** Your mouth, when food is properly chewed!

Abbreviations and Equivalents

ABBREVIATIONS

cm = centimeter

fl. oz. = fluid ounce

ft. = foot

gm = gram

in. = inch

kg = kilogram

L = liter

lb. = pound

ml = milliliter

mm = millimeter

oz. = ounce

qt. = quart

tbsp. = tablespoon

tsp. = teaspoon

EQUIVALENTS

2 tbsp. = 30 ml = 1 fl. oz.

¼ cup = 60 ml = 2 fl. oz.

⅓ cup = 80 ml = 3 fl. oz.

½ cup = 125 ml = 4 fl. oz.

⅔ cup = 160 ml = 5 fl. oz.

¾ cup = 180 ml = 6 fl. oz.

1 cup = 250 ml = 8 fl. oz.

1½ cups = 375 ml = 12 fl. oz.

2 cups = 500 ml = 16 fl. oz.

Lose Weight

WATERMELON JUICE

If you have ever tasted a watermelon, it is probably no surprise to you how this juicy, refreshing fruit got its name. Watermelon has an extremely high water content—a whopping 92 percent. Its high-quality water content makes it an excellent cleanser and detoxifier for the whole body. This sweet, juicy fruit is packed with some of the most important **antioxidants** in nature. (Antioxidants are compounds that protect against oxidative stress that can lead to cellular damage.) It is an excellent source of **vitamin C** and a very good source of **vitamin A.** Pink watermelon contains the potent carotenoid antioxidant **lycopene.** Watermelon is not only great on a hot summer day, the nutrients in this delectable fruit may also help reduce the inflammation that contributes to conditions like asthma, atherosclerosis, diabetes, colon cancer, and arthritis. Because watermelon has a higher water content and lower calorie content than most other fruits (1 cup of watermelon contains only 48 calories), it delivers more nutrients per calorie, making it an outstanding health value.

MAKES 32–48 OUNCES

1 (27–30-inch) watermelon

Cut the watermelon in half vertically. Scoop out the flesh (including the seeds, which are high in protein, iron, and calcium) with a large spoon and place it into a blender. Blend on high for 5 minutes or until the seeds are pulverized. If you can hear the seeds hitting the sides of the blender jar, process the watermelon a little longer. If the blades of the blender take more than five seconds to begin spinning (once the watermelon is in the blender), add a small amount of fresh spring water (no more than 1/4 cup) to facilitate blending.

Strain the juice into a bowl or glass, and discard any pulp that remains in the strainer. If the juice doesn't flow freely through the strainer, stir it with a spoon or a fork to help the juice move through the pulp. Serve at once or chill the juice in the refrigerator for 10–20 minutes.

Vegetable Combo One

One of the oldest and most versatile of the healing herbs, dandelion is regarded as a liver tonic, diuretic, and blood cleanser. This is due to its content of **mucilages,** which soothe the digestive tract, absorb toxins from ingested food, and regulate intestinal bacteria. Dandelion leaves have a bitter, slightly astringent flavor. While these greens are available all year long, they are at their peak of flavor and nutrition in early spring. Young dandelion leaves will be more tender and less bitter than larger, more mature ones. Add raw dandelion greens to salads, cook them like spinach, or add a few leaves when you juice your favorite vegetables. Dandelion greens are a good source of **calcium, iron,** and **vitamins A and C.**

Beets are one of nature's best bodily cleansers and detoxifiers. Their natural sugars make them deliciously sweet. Beets are an excellent source of **folate** and a good source of **potassium** and **vitamin C**.

MAKES 24 OUNCES

2-3 carrots, juiced

1 cup spring water or distilled water

½–1 lemon, juiced

¼ beet, juiced

Pinch of dandelion (see note)

Combine all the ingredients in a blender and process until smooth.

Note: Dandelion is available in several forms: dried leaf, dried root, tea, extract (a powdered or liquid extract prepared from the roots, leaves, and flowers), and fresh leaves. A tea can be made from the dried root or from fresh leaves. For fresh tea, simply steam the fresh leaves like spinach and use the liquid they express as a tea. Any form of dandelion may be used in this recipe.

PURIFICATION

Although acidic to the taste, lemons have a strong **alkaline** reaction in the body. They destroy putrefactive bacteria in both the intestines and mouth, and alleviate flatulence and indigestion in general. Lemons are an outstanding source of **vitamin C,** but much of this valuable vitamin is lost if the juice is left exposed to air or stored for very long. The cayenne in this recipe is an essential ingredient, as it helps stimulate circulation, perspiration, and digestion.

MAKES 1 GALLON

> **6 lemons, juiced**
>
> **14 cups spring water (1 gallon minus 2 cups)**
>
> **1 cup pure maple syrup**
>
> **½ teaspoon cayenne**

Strain the lemon juice and add it to the water along with the maple syrup and cayenne. Seal with a lid and shake well. Store leftovers in a tightly sealed container in the refrigerator.

Note: The easiest way to make this beverage is directly in the gallon jug for the spring water. Just remove 2 cups of spring water from the jug and set it aside for another use. Add the remaining ingredients to the water remaining in the jug, put on the cap, and shake well.

Cleanse Your System

DETOXIFICATION

Citrus fruits work as strong **solvents** in the body, stimulating the liver and gallbladder, and stirring up toxic settlements that cannot be eliminated any other way.

MAKES 2–2½ CUPS

> 2 oranges, juiced
>
> 1 grapefruit, juiced
>
> 1 cup ice (optional)
>
> 2 lemons, juiced
>
> ¼ cup pure maple syrup

Combine all the ingredients in a blender and process for about 1 minute.

DAILY GRAPE DRINK

The secret is out! Grapes are powerful **detoxifiers** that can cleanse and purify your system. Similar to watermelon, grapes are a natural **diuretic,** drawing toxins from the body. They are also a principal source of **vitamin P,** also known as **bioflavonoids.** Flavonoids are compounds found in fruits, vegetables, and certain beverages; they have diverse, beneficial biochemical and antioxidant effects.

MAKES 24–32 OUNCES

1 pound black grapes, with seeds

Blend the grapes until liquefied. Strain if desired. Chill for 10–15 minutes before serving.

Note: A diet consisting solely of grape juice is not recommended. Drink one glass per day as a part of your daily regimen.

Strengthen Your Immune System

FRESH QUENCH

Grapefruits were discovered relatively recently, in Barbados in the 18th century. The name reflects the way the fruit is arranged when it grows—hanging in clusters, just like grapes.

MAKES 16–24 OUNCES

> 5 oranges, juiced
>
> 1 grapefruit, juiced
>
> 2 lemons, juiced
>
> 1/2 cup ice (optional)
>
> 1/4 cup pure maple syrup

Pour the juices into a blender. Add the optional ice and maple syrup. Blend for 4 minutes, or until the ice is pulverized.

GINGER GET WELL

Here is a natural way to ward off colds, especially during the change of seasons. Ginger is held in high regard in many traditional cuisines. This spicy root **strengthens the immune system** and **aids in blood circulation.** It also may also help to **lower blood pressure** and **reduce LDL ("bad") cholesterol.**

MAKES ABOUT 32 OUNCES

> **2 pieces fresh gingerroot (each piece about 6 inches long; peeling is optional), juiced or very finely chopped**
>
> **1 cup pineapple cubes**
>
> **1 orange, juiced**
>
> **½ cup ice**
>
> **⅓ cup pure maple syrup or raw organic honey**
>
> **1 teaspoon ground nutmeg**

Combine all the ingredients in a blender and process until smooth.

Note: The gingerroot may need to be cut in half lengthwise in order for it to fit into your juicer. If you prefer, 1 cup natural ginger juice drink (available in natural food stores) may be used in place of the fresh gingerroot.

VEGETABLE COMBO TWO

Carotenoids are natural fat-soluble pigments found principally in plants. They are responsible for many of the red, orange, and yellow hues of plant leaves, fruits, and flowers. Some familiar examples of carotenoid coloration are the oranges of carrots and citrus fruits, and the reds of peppers and tomatoes. Over six hundred different carotenoids are known to occur naturally, and new carotenoids continue to be identified. **Beta-carotene,** found in carrots and other yellow-orange vegetables, is one of approximately fifty carotenoids that are called "provitamin A" compounds, because the body can convert them into retinol, an active form of **vitamin A.** Long-term inadequate intake of carotenoids is associated with chronic disease, including heart disease and various cancers. Carotenoids found in foods, not supplements, may play a role in the prevention of age-related macular degeneration, cataracts, asthma, cervical dysplasia, chlamydial infection, heart disease, lung cancer, male and female infertility, osteoarthritis, prostate cancer, skin cancer, vaginal candidiasis, and others. Serve this delicious, health-supporting beverage several times a week. A small amount of **echinacea** (useful for its infection-fighting abilities) or **spirulina powder** may be added prior to blending.

MAKES 24 OUNCES

> 6 carrots, juiced
>
> 2–4 pieces fresh gingerroot (each piece about 6 inches long; peeling is optional), juiced, or 1 cup natural ginger juice drink (available in natural food stores)

Stir, shake, or blend the juices until well combined.

Increase Your Energy Level

Feeling tired, sluggish, or depressed? These may be warning signs that your body needs "fuel" fast, or that it is overloaded with toxic substances that need to be eliminated. While sugary snacks and processed foods are handy and can give us a quick boost, they will put us on an energy roller coaster. That rapid surge will be followed by a swift crash, making us feel even worse than before. For maximum energy, we need plenty of water, sea vegetables, nuts, green veggies, and a variety of fresh fruit every day.

EVERLASTING LIFE

Tahini, a paste made from ground sesame seeds, is a rich source of healthy fats and an excellent source of protein. Spirulina is an aquatic plant, blue-green in color and rich in **chlorophyll, minerals,** and **amino acids.** Kelp, like many sea vegetables, is a good source of **iodine** and helps to fight the harmful effects of radiation. Wheat germ is a good source of **vitamin E, folic acid,** and **iron.** Make sure the protein powder you use in this recipe is totally plant-based and does not contain any dairy products or animal derivatives. If you use the banana, it is rich in **potassium,** the "sister" mineral of sodium. Potassium helps maintain nerve and muscle impulses, as well as balance water in the body.

MAKES 16 OUNCES

> 1 ripe banana (optional)
>
> 1 cup ice
>
> 1/4 cup pure maple syrup
>
> 1 tablespoon tahini
>
> 1 teaspoon spirulina powder
>
> 1 teaspoon kelp powder
>
> 1 teaspoon vegetarian protein powder
>
> 1 teaspoon wheat germ

Combine all the ingredients in a blender and process until smooth.

Quick-Me-Up

Strawberries are an excellent source of **vitamin C** and **folate.** They are also packed with powerful **antioxidants** that provide protection by neutralizing free radicals—substances in the body that can damage cells and lead to disease. Strawberries may help protect the brain from oxidative stress and may reduce the effects of age-related declines in brain function. Apples provide respectable amounts of both insoluble and soluble **fiber** (including pectin), some **vitamin C,** and **potassium.** Apples are also a good source of **quercetin,** a flavonoid that may help protect against heart disease. Bananas can be easily digested by nearly everyone, including infants and the elderly. This tropical fruit supplies a substantial amount of **potassium** along with significant amounts of **vitamin B$_6$.**

MAKES 24 OUNCES

- 1 red apple, washed, cored, and quartered (peeling is optional)
- 1 cup coconut milk, almond milk, rice milk, or soymilk
- 1 cup ice
- 1 ripe banana
- 1/4 cup pure maple syrup
- 4 strawberries
- 1 teaspoon vegetarian protein powder

Place all the ingredients in a blender and process until smooth.

THE RESURRECTION

Soy is an excellent source of high-quality **protein.** It also is prized for its high levels of **essential fatty acids,** numerous **vitamins** and **minerals,** and **isoflavones,** which may help reduce the risk of cardiovascular disease. This creamy, soy-based shake makes a delicious way to boost energy levels.

MAKES 16 OUNCES

> 2 cups carob or vanilla soy ice cream
>
> 1 cup carob soymilk
>
> 1 tablespoon spirulina powder

Combine all the ingredients in a blender and process for 4–7 seconds.

VEGETABLE COMBO THREE

Kale is an excellent source of several important nutrients, including **vitamins A, C,** and **B$_6$,** and **manganese.** The manganese in kale helps produce energy from protein and carbohydrates. Kale is also a very good source of dietary **fiber, calcium, copper, iron,** and **vitamins B$_1$, B$_2$,** and **E.** This combination of vitamins, minerals, and phytonutrients makes kale a nutrition superstar!

MAKES 24 OUNCES

> 3 carrots
>
> 2 leaves kale or collard greens, very finely chopped
>
> 2 cups spring water or distilled water
>
> 1/4 cup lemon juice
>
> 1/4 cup pure maple syrup
>
> 1 teaspoon spirulina powder
>
> 1/2 teaspoon kelp powder (optional)

Juice the carrots and greens in a vegetable juicer. Transfer the juice to a blender and add the remaining ingredients. Process for 4–6 minutes.

Elevate Your Mood

PICK-ME-UP COCONUT DATE SHAKE

Exercise brings more oxygen to our brain cells, making us feel energized and happy. Foods rich in **iron,** such as dates and blackstrap molasses, also help transport oxygen to our cells, elevating our energy level and mood. Iron-rich foods and exercise complement each other perfectly.

MAKES 20 OUNCES

> 1 cup coconut milk or vanilla soymilk
>
> 1 cup ice
>
> 10 pitted dates
>
> 1/4 cup raw almonds, cashews, or walnuts, soaked overnight and drained
>
> 1 teaspoon blackstrap molasses
>
> 1/4 teaspoon vanilla extract (optional)
>
> 1/8 teaspoon ground cinnamon
>
> 1/8 teaspoon ground nutmeg

Combine all the ingredients in a blender and process until smooth.

FRUITY ICE CREAM SOY SHAKE

A shake that tastes great and is great for us—what more could we ask for? Enjoy it with a smile.

MAKES ABOUT 24 OUNCES

> 3 cups vanilla soy ice cream
>
> ¼ cup blueberries, ripe mango, or pineapple cubes, or 4 strawberries
>
> 1 cup rice milk, almond milk, or vanilla soymilk
>
> ¼ cup pure maple syrup (optional)

Combine all the ingredients in a blender and process until smooth.

Mango Melody

Mangoes, peaches, lemons, and oranges are packed with essential **vitamins, phytochemicals,** and other vital nutrients that help prevent and fight infection.

MAKES 32 OUNCES

> 2 oranges, juiced
>
> 1/2 ripe mango
>
> 1/2 ripe peach
>
> 1/3 cup ice
>
> 1/4 cup pure maple syrup
>
> 2 tablespoons lemon juice

Combine all the ingredients in a blender and process just until slushy.

VEGETABLE COMBO FOUR

What do kale, collards, alfalfa, and spinach have in common? They all are excellent sources of **vitamins C** and **A, iron,** and **chlorophyll.** Foods rich in **beta-carotene,** such as carrots, help repair tissue and replenish cells. The juice of young barley plants (available in liquid, powder, or tablet form) contains a variety of minerals, including **potassium, calcium,** and **magnesium.**

MAKES 28 OUNCES

> **6 carrots**
>
> **1 cup finely chopped spinach**
>
> **½ cup finely chopped alfalfa sprouts**
>
> **¼ cup liquid barley juice, or 1 tablespoon barley juice powder**
>
> **2 tablespoons lemon juice (optional)**

Juice the carrots and the spinach in a vegetable juicer. Transfer the juice to a blender. Add the remaining ingredients and process for 4–6 minutes. Strain before serving.

Increase Your Stamina

The mastery of a skill is not measured solely by our ability to perform a certain task but by our ability to maintain that task for a prolonged period of time. Stamina does not mean speed; it means endurance. The proverb about the race not being given to the swift but to those who endure must have been written about the wise people who decided to add the following shakes to their diet.

LAST MAN (OR WOMAN) STANDING

Nuts and seeds provide the body with valuable **protein, zinc, and essential fats** that help regenerate cells and tissues and maintain a healthy, balanced system. Be sure to soak nuts and seeds overnight or for at least eight to twelve hours before consuming them, as this will enhance their nutrient content and digestibility. If you want to live forever, or at least feel as though you will, give your body the nutrients it needs to stay the course!

MAKES 32 OUNCES

> 2 cups spring water
>
> 1/2 cup raw sesame or pumpkin seeds, soaked overnight and drained
>
> 1 1/2 teaspoons blackstrap molasses
>
> 1 teaspoon spirulina powder
>
> 1 teaspoon kelp powder
>
> 1 teaspoon vegetarian protein powder
>
> 1 teaspoon brewer's yeast or wheat germ
>
> 1/8 teaspoon ground cinnamon
>
> 1/8 teaspoon ground nutmeg
>
> 1 cup ice
>
> 1/2 cup pure maple syrup

Combine the water, seeds, molasses, spirulina powder, kelp powder, protein powder, brewer's yeast, cinnamon, and nutmeg in a blender. Process for 2 minutes. Add the ice and maple syrup and process for 1 minute longer.

Pineapple Supreme Piña Colada

Pineapples are considered nature's preventative health care cabinet. This is because pineapple contains an enzyme called **bromelain,** which is particularly useful for reducing muscle and tissue inflammation and as a digestive aid. Supplements are made from the enzymes found in the pineapple stem. Bromelain works by breaking down a blood-clotting protein that can impede good circulation and prevent tissues from draining properly. Bromelain also blocks the production of compounds that can cause swelling and pain. Pineapples also are an excellent source of **vitamin C,** as are oranges.

MAKES 16 OUNCES

> 2 cups coconut milk
> 1 orange, juiced
> ½ cup pineapple cubes
> ½ cup pure maple syrup
> ½ cup ice

Combine all the ingredients in a blender and process until completely smooth.

VEGETABLE COMBO FIVE

Bee pollen is collected by beekeepers from the supplies that bees have extracted from the flowers of certain plants. It has been prized by health enthusiasts for its varying amounts of **protein, B vitamins, carbohydrates, amino acids,** and **enzymes.**

The sweet taste of beets reflects their high sugar content. They have the highest sugar content of all vegetables, yet they are very low in calories. This colorful root vegetable contains powerful nutrient compounds that help protect against heart disease and birth defects. The pigment that gives beets their rich, purple-crimson color—**betacyanin**—is also a powerful cancer-fighting agent.

MAKES 16–24 OUNCES

> 4 carrots, juiced
> ¼ beet, juiced
> 2 lettuce leaves, finely chopped
> 1 teaspoon bee pollen

Combine all the ingredients in a blender and process for 4 minutes. Strain before serving.

Memory, Clarity, and Focus

Many aspects of life help to shape our intellectual, emotional, and psychological growth and development. When these influences are positive, they can have a beneficial impact on us. When they are negative, their effect can be harmful and damaging. Fortunately, our bodies and minds are resilient, and once we replace negative habits and activities with valuable life-affirming and health-supporting choices, our mental health will parallel our physical well-being.

PEACH DELIVERANCE

Mangoes, peaches, pineapples, and other fruits and vegetables that are rich in **vitamin C** help our bodies fight infection. When we are free of infection and ill health, we are able to concentrate on other important aspects of life. All seekers of optimum health know the valuable connection between a healthy body and a focused mind.

MAKES 16 OUNCES

> 1 cup pineapple juice
>
> 1 ripe peach
>
> ½ orange, juiced
>
> ½ cup ice
>
> ¼ cup pure maple syrup

Combine all the ingredients in a blender and process until smooth.

SECOND RESURRECTION

Bananas are one of our best sources of **potassium,** an essential mineral for maintaining normal blood pressure and heart function. Since the average banana contains an impressive 467 milligrams of potassium and only 1 milligram of sodium, a banana a day could help to prevent high blood pressure and protect against atherosclerosis. The potassium found in bananas may also help to promote bone health. Potassium counteracts the increased urinary calcium loss caused by the high-salt diets typical of most people, thus helping to slow down or prevent thinning bones.

Spirulina is one of the highest sources of **protein, beta-carotene,** and **nucleic acids** of any food—plant or animal. All of its nutrients are in a form that is easily digested and absorbed.

MAKES 24 OUNCES

> **2 ripe bananas**
>
> **1 cup almond milk, rice milk, or soymilk**
>
> **¼ cup pure maple syrup**
>
> **1 tablespoon spirulina powder**

Combine all the ingredients in a blender and process until smooth.

Cucumber Lemonade

The phrase "cool as a cucumber" makes much good sense. This vegetable's high water content gives it a very unique moist and refreshing taste. While the flesh of cucumbers is primarily composed of water, it also contains two compounds that help prevent water retention: ascorbic acid (**vitamin C**) and **caffeic acid** (a natural **antioxidant** found in fruits and vegetables; it is not related to caffeine). The hard skin of cucumbers is rich in fiber and contains a variety of beneficial minerals including **silica, potassium,** and **magnesium.**

MAKES 32–48 OUNCES

4 cucumbers, chopped

4 lemons, juiced

1/2 cup ice

1/4 cup pure maple syrup

Combine all the ingredients in a blender and process until smooth.

Vegetable Combo Six

Cucumbers are an **alkaline,** nonstarchy, cooling vegetable, rich in minerals that neutralize blood acidosis. Considered the best natural **diuretic** known, cucumbers facilitate the excretion of wastes through the kidneys and help to dissolve uric accumulations (such as kidney and bladder stones). Rich in **enzymes,** the cucumber is also a beneficial digestive aid.

MAKES 16–24 OUNCES

4 cucumbers

Wash the cucumbers but do not peel. Juice the cucumbers in a vegetable juicer. Alternatively, coarsely chop the cucumbers, and then process them into a liquid in a blender. Strain and let chill in the freezer for 10 minutes before serving.

Relax Your Nerves

ETERNITY WINTER

To relax jittery nerves or settle a queasy stomach, give cinnamon a try. Cinnamon contains **catechins,** which are **flavonoid** phytochemical compounds that aid relaxation and quell nausea. The powerful **antioxidant** properties of catechins also neutralize free radicals, which can lead to the development of cancer. In addition, catechins may inhibit the formation of cancer-causing substances in the body, enhance the body's natural anticancer defenses, and block the growth of cancer cells. Green tea, grapes, olives, pears, barley, and many other nutritious foods also contain catechins.

MAKES ABOUT 28 OUNCES (2 MEDIUM MUGS)

- **2 cups almond milk**
- **¼ cup pure maple syrup**
- **2 tablespoons carob powder**
- **⅛ teaspoon ground cinnamon**
- **⅛ teaspoon ground nutmeg**
- **2 cups vanilla or toasted almond soy ice cream (optional)**

Combine the almond milk, maple syrup, carob powder, cinnamon, and nutmeg in a small saucepan. Warm over medium-low heat until steaming hot. Do not boil. Add the optional soy ice cream, remove from the heat, and stir until liquefied and well combined. Enjoy this beverage with a spoon.

Hebrew Sunrise

Oranges, pineapples, and mangoes supply plenty of **vitamin C,** which is best known as a cell protector, immunity booster, and powerful antioxidant. The body's ligaments, tendons, and collagen (a protein found in connective tissues) rely on the presence of vitamin C to stay strong and healthy. Like all antioxidants, vitamin C counters the effects of cell-damaging free radicals. As an added benefit, it even helps the body recycle other antioxidants.

In addition to providing vitamin C, mangoes are a splendid source of **beta-carotene,** as their vivid orange flesh would suggest. They also supply some **vitamin B$_6$** and even some **vitamin E.**

Lecithin, a fatty substance manufactured in the body, is widely found in many plant-based foods, including peanuts, soybeans, and wheat germ. It is considered an excellent source of **choline,** one of the B vitamins. Once in the body, a key component of lecithin—**phosphatidylcholine**—breaks down into choline. Phosphatidylcholine (PC) might be thought of as a purified extract of lecithin. It is commonly recommended for treating liver, nerve, and a variety of other conditions, including multiple sclerosis and memory loss. Liquid lecithin is available at most natural food stores.

MAKES ABOUT 32 OUNCES

> 2 cups pineapple juice
>
> 1½ cups ice
>
> 1 orange
>
> ½ ripe mango
>
> ⅓ cup pure maple syrup
>
> 1½ teaspoons liquid lecithin

Combine all the ingredients in a blender and process until smooth.

Balance Your Being

LEMONADE

A surprising number and variety of physical problems and diseases can be caused by an overly **acidic** diet. Many people in industrialized nations today suffer from health problems caused by our modern lifestyle and, most significant, a diet of refined and processed foods, which promotes acidification of the body's internal environment. Acidifying elements include proteins, cereals, and sugars. **Alkaline** foods, such as vegetables, often are eaten in much smaller quantities, and their alkaline content is insufficient to neutralize surplus acids. Stimulants—such as tobacco, coffee, tea, and alcohol—are extremely acidifying. Stress and physical activity (both in insufficient or excessive amounts) can also cause acidification. Despite their sour taste, lemons become alkaline once they are ingested. This simple but delicious lemonade can help restore our body's **health-supporting** alkaline environment, so drink it often.

MAKES 24 OUNCES

> 4 small lemons, juiced
> 2 cups spring water or distilled water
> ½ cup ice
> ¼ cup pure maple syrup

Strain the lemon juice and transfer it to a blender. Add the remaining ingredients and process until well combined.

TROPICAL COOLER

When our body feels out of balance, it's usually a sign that it needs a good rest. Sometimes we just need a respite from heavier foods, such as starches, fats, and dense protein foods (including nuts and seeds). Fruit is light and contains a wealth of **vitamins, minerals, phytochemicals,** and **antioxidants** that are essential to keep us functioning at optimum levels. Most of us don't consume enough fresh fruit or a wide assortment of it. This delicious recipe will help you solve that problem with ease and joy.

MAKES 24 OUNCES

> 1 cup pineapple juice
>
> 1/2 cup ice
>
> 1 kiwi (peeling is optional)
>
> 4 strawberries
>
> 1/4 cup pineapple cubes
>
> 1/4 cup pure maple syrup
>
> 1 cup vanilla soy ice cream (optional)

Combine the pineapple juice, ice, kiwi, strawberries, pineapple cubes, and maple syrup in a blender. Process until completely smooth. Add the optional soy ice cream and process just until creamy. Serve at once or chill in the freezer until frosty. Serve with a spoon.

Protein
Power

Our bodies require protein just like plants require water. While an excess of protein (or an excess of anything, for that matter) should be avoided, we need to maintain healthy protein levels. One way to ensure adequate protein is to avoid sugary snack foods and highly processed items, and balance our intake of fresh fruits, vegetables, nuts, seeds, beans, and whole grains.

Hazelnut Heaven

Hazelnuts are delicious and nutrient dense, providing us with excellent nourishment. The **monounsaturated fats** in nuts are believed to lower LDL ("bad") cholesterol levels. When compared with other nuts, hazelnuts have a high **vitamin E** profile. Current research indicates that the antioxidant power of vitamin E may play a significant role in preventing heart disease and certain kinds of cancer. Hazelnuts are also rich in **phosphorus, potassium, copper, zinc, magnesium, selenium, dietary fiber, folate,** and **plant sterols,** which are believed to play a role in the prevention of certain diseases, including colon cancer and heart disease.

MAKES ABOUT 24 OUNCES

> 1 cup almond milk
>
> 1/3 cup hazelnuts, soaked overnight and drained
>
> 1/4 cup pure maple syrup
>
> 1 tablespoon blackstrap molasses
>
> 1/8 teaspoon ground cinnamon
>
> 1/8 teaspoon vanilla extract (optional)
>
> 1 ripe banana
>
> 1 cup ice

Combine the almond milk, hazelnuts, maple syrup, blackstrap molasses, cinnamon, and optional vanilla extract in a blender and process until smooth. Add the banana and ice and blend again until creamy.

PROTEIN SHAKE FOR
STRONG NAILS, HAIR, AND SKIN

Oats are native to the warm Mediterranean regions and have been cultivated for thousands of years as a source of food and folk remedies. Oats are famous for the nutritious cereal grain we cook for our morning oatmeal. The herb known as **oat straw** refers to the whole oat plant, including the leaves and stems. These parts of the plant are dried and chopped and then used both internally and externally by traditional herbalists. In traditional medicine, oat straw is used in various forms to treat a number of ailments, including arthritis and rheumatism; it's also taken as a diuretic tea to combat fluid retention. Oat straw is a concentrated source of **silica** (silicon dioxide), which is key to the development of healthy skin, hair, nails, and bones. Look for oat straw at your natural food store.

MAKES 16 OUNCES

    1½ cups ice

    1 cup almond milk

    1 ripe banana

    ¼ cup pure maple syrup

    1 tablespoon vegetarian protein powder

    1 tablespoon oat straw

    ⅛ teaspoon ground cinnamon

Combine all the ingredients in a blender and process until smooth.

Vegetable Combo Seven

Spinach is exceptionally rich in **carotenoids,** including **beta-carotene** and **lutein.** It also contains **quercetin,** a flavonoid phytochemical with antioxidant properties. Spinach is rich in vitamins and minerals, particularly **folate** (folic acid), **vitamin K, magnesium,** and **manganese;** it also contains more **protein** than most other vegetables.

MAKES 16 OUNCES

> 1 cucumber, coarsely chopped (do not peel)
>
> 1 cup spinach, finely chopped
>
> 1/2 cup green peas (optional)
>
> 1/2 lemon, juiced
>
> 1 teaspoon spirulina powder
>
> 1/2 small clove garlic, chopped

Combine all the ingredients in a blender and process until smooth. Strain before serving.

Revive Your System

CRANBERRY CRUNCH

It has long been believed that cranberries prevent or cure urinary tract infection (UTI) by acidifying the urine, thus creating an inhospitable environment for the bacteria usually responsible for UTIs. Recent research, however, has disclosed that condensed tannins, called **proanthocyanidins,** are the compounds in cranberries responsible for preventing and treating UTIs. Rather than making the urine more acid, they work by preventing the bacteria from binding to the wall of the urinary tract, rendering the bacteria harmless.

In addition to their principal role in combating urinary tract infections, cranberries may also have broad-spectrum antibiotic value against E. coli and other harmful bacteria. Dentists have discovered that cranberries and cranberry juice contain specific compounds that can block the formation of dental plaque and potentially lessen tooth decay and gum disease. Current research indicates that cranberry juice may help keep LDL ("bad") cholesterol from oxidizing, which suggests that cranberries may offer a natural defense against atherosclerosis.

These healthful, tart little berries are an excellent source of **vitamins A** and **C** and **potassium.** Although cranberries contain some tannins, they will not interfere with the absorption of minerals. Additionally, cranberries appear to enhance the absorption of **vitamin B$_{12}$.**

MAKES 16 OUNCES

1 cup vanilla soymilk, rice milk, or almond milk

1 cup vanilla soy ice cream (optional)

$\frac{1}{2}$ cup cranberries

$\frac{1}{2}$ cup ice

$\frac{1}{4}$ cup pure maple syrup

1 tablespoon granola

Combine the soymilk, optional soy ice cream, cranberries, ice, and maple syrup in a blender, and process until smooth and creamy. Eat at once or briefly chill in the freezer until frosty. Sprinkle with the granola and eat with a spoon.

REHYDRATION DRINK

When you are exposed to excessive heat, don't drink enough water, or engage in intense activity, your body can become dehydrated. When you are thirsty and your mouth feels dry, you've already entered the early stages of dehydration. You should always drink sufficient water on a regular basis so that you never allow yourself to become parched. On those occasions that you do, however, this tonic will help replenish your system.

MAKES 24 OUNCES

> **2 cups spring water**
>
> **6 lemons or oranges, juiced**
>
> **¼ cup pure maple syrup**
>
> **1 teaspoon kelp powder**
>
> **½ teaspoon sea salt**

Combine all the ingredients in a blender and process just until well combined.

VERY BERRY FINE

Berries are among nature's most potent health foods. They are rich in **vitamin C,** a nutrient that is vital to the production of **collagen,** which is involved in the building and health of cartilage, joints, skin, and blood vessels. Vitamin C boosts our immune system by fighting off foreign invaders, neutralizing pollutants, providing natural antihistamines, and shielding fatty acids from oxidation. The **fiber** in berries may help protect against colon cancer, reduce the risk of heart disease by lowering "bad" cholesterol levels, regulate blood sugar levels, and control appetite by creating a feeling of fullness. The **phytochemicals** in berries help prevent cancer, heart disease, diabetes, high blood pressure, and could possibly reverse the effects of aging by improving memory and motor skills.

Papayas are a rich source of antioxidant nutrients such as **carotenes, vitamin C,** and **flavonoids.** They are also abundant in the B vitamins **folate** and **pantothenic acid;** the minerals **potassium** and **magnesium;** and **fiber.** Together, these nutrients promote the health of the cardiovascular system and also provide protection against colon cancer. In addition, papaya contains the digestive enzyme **papain,** which aids digestion.

MAKES 16 OUNCES

> 1 cup papaya juice
>
> ¼ cup pure maple syrup
>
> ¼ cup blueberries
>
> ¼ cup sliced strawberries (about 4)
>
> ¼ cup ice
>
> 1 tablespoon cranberries

Combine all the ingredients in a blender and process until smooth. Serve at once or chill briefly in the refrigerator.

VEGETABLE COMBO EIGHT

Carrots are an excellent source of antioxidant compounds, which protect against cardiovascular disease and cancer and also promote good vision, especially night vision. Kale and collard greens have an abundance of **vitamins A** and **C** as well as several of the **B-complex vitamins.** They are good sources of important minerals, including **calcium, potassium, phosphorus, manganese, magnesium,** and **iron.** What's more, these beautiful, dark leafy greens contribute essential **omega-3 fatty acids.**

Sea vegetables, such as spirulina, provide **folic acid** and are a very good source of **magnesium,** which has been shown to lower high blood pressure and reduce the risk of heart attack. They also contain **pantothenic acid** and **riboflavin**—two B vitamins necessary for energy production. The unique combination of ingredients in this colorful tonic are sure to give your mind and body a boost.

MAKES 16 OUNCES

> **3 carrots, juiced**
>
> **1 cucumber, juiced**
>
> **1 cup finely chopped kale or collard greens, juiced**
>
> **1 tablespoon lemon juice**
>
> **1 teaspoon spirulina powder**
>
> **½ cup ice (optional)**

Combine the juices and spirulina powder in a blender. Add the optional ice and process for 2 minutes. Strain. If the ice is omitted, chill the strained mixture for 10 minutes in the freezer before serving.

Master Your Mornings!

To get your system moving in the morning, the first thing you should have is water. After that, eating fruit early in the day will help to sustain your body. Instead of gulping a cup of coffee or eating a heavy breakfast loaded with fat or refined carbohydrates, drink a fresh fruit shake to get energized and keep going until lunchtime!

BANANA BREEZE

Bananas and strawberries are good sources of **potassium, antioxidants,** and **pectin,** a soluble fiber that absorbs fluid, thus helping to normalize movement through the digestive tract and ease constipation. In bananas, pectin is combined with a good supply of **starch,** providing **complex carbohydrates** for slow-burning energy.

MAKES 32 OUNCES

- 2 ripe bananas
- 1 cup soymilk or coconut milk
- 1 cup ice
- 8 strawberries
- 1/2 cup pure maple syrup
- 1/2 cup pineapple cubes pineapple juice

Combine all the ingredients in a blender and process until smooth and creamy. Serve at once or chill briefly in the refrigerator.

OAT BREAKFAST SHAKE

Remember those hardy, old-fashioned breakfasts when Mom served hot oatmeal? She was on the right track! Oats are great for our total well-being. They are an excellent source of the complex carbohydrates that help us sustain energy. They also contain about twice as much protein as brown rice. Oats offer impressive levels of **thiamin, phosphorus,** and **manganese,** and respectable quantities of **copper, folate** (folic acid), **vitamin E,** and **zinc.** The soluble **fiber** in oats has been credited with helping to lower blood cholesterol levels and stabilize blood sugar. In addition to its fiber benefits, oats are a very good source of **selenium,** which works with vitamin E in numerous vital antioxidant systems throughout the body. These powerful antioxidant actions make selenium helpful in decreasing asthma symptoms and in the prevention of heart disease. Selenium is also involved in DNA repair and is associated with a reduced risk of cancer, especially colon cancer. For a super start to your day, this recipe is a great alternative to hot oatmeal.

MAKES 32 OUNCES

> 1 ripe banana
>
> ½ cup rolled oats soaked in ½ cup spring water for 2 to 4 minutes
>
> ½ cup ice
>
> 8 strawberries
>
> ¼ cup pure maple syrup

Combine all the ingredients in a blender and process until smooth and creamy.

Make Your Your Children Smile

FRESH FREEZE

We always want to be sure that we give our children the best, but in today's world "the best" is often imitated, but never duplicated, by processed, preserved, and packaged "food." This quick, fresh treat offers a double blessing: It's a relief for you to know that your children are truly getting the best and most wholesome foods; and it's a delight for little ones because it is so delicious. You can make this recipe using a variety of your choice of fresh fruits—feel free to experiment.

MAKES ABOUT 4 SERVINGS

Bottom Layer:

>   1 cup pineapple juice
>   8 strawberries
>   1/2 cup pineapple cubes
>   1/4 cup pure maple syrup

Combine all the ingredients in a blender and process until slushy. Pour into four cups or mugs, filling each about three-quarters full.

Top Layer:

>   4 strawberries
>   1/4 cup pineapple cubes
>   2 tablespoons pure maple syrup

Combine all the ingredients in a blender and process until slushy. Pour over the bottom layer. Serve with a spoon.

KIWI LEMONADE

Whether it's a hot summer day or the middle of winter, lemonade is always refreshing. Lemons are an alkalizing fruit that aids digestion. One kiwifruit contains our daily requirement of **vitamin C.** Kiwis are also high in **vitamin K** and provide a good source of fiber and potassium. They help to neutralize free radicals due to the presence of both **vitamin C** and **antioxidant flavonoids** such as **catechins.** A lesser-known fact is that kiwis contain **actinidin,** an **enzyme** with physical and chemical properties similar to those of papain in papaya, which assists digestion.

MAKES 32 OUNCES

> 2 cups spring water or distilled water
>
> 8 lemons, juiced
>
> 1 cup ice
>
> 2 kiwifruit, peeled
>
> 1/2 cup pure maple syrup or "raw" cane sugar

Combine all the ingredients in a blender. For a slushy consistency, blend for 10 seconds. For a juicelike consistency, blend until completely smooth.

Increase Body Mass

If you'd like to put on a few healthy pounds, include one of these rich, delicious shakes in your daily diet. Although these shakes won't do the trick alone, they certainly will give you a head start, if that's your goal.

TROPICAL DREAM

This thick shake is incredibly creamy and so rich tasting you won't believe it's a "health drink."

MAKES 24 OUNCES

> 1 ripe banana
>
> 1 cup ice
>
> ½ cup pineapple juice or pineapple cubes
>
> ½ cup coconut milk
>
> ½ cup pure maple syrup
>
> 4 strawberries

Combine all the ingredients in a blender and process for 1 minute.

Banana Moon

Bananas are powerhouses of nutritional energy. They are comprised of 76 percent water, 20 percent sugar, 12 percent starch, a large number of vitamins and minerals, and **fiber.** The high vitamin and mineral content (especially **potassium**) of bananas benefits the muscular and nervous systems, and the natural sugars in bananas are readily assimilated for use as fuel.

MAKES 32 OUNCES

> 2 ripe bananas
>
> 2 cups ice
>
> 1 cup almond milk or vanilla soymilk
>
> 1 cup vanilla soy ice cream
>
> ¼ cup pure maple syrup
>
> 1½ teaspoons blackstrap molasses

Combine all the ingredients in a blender and process just until smooth and creamy. Do not overprocess or the mixture will become too thin.

Fruit Salads, Pie, and Pudding

While juices are easy to prepare, drink, and digest, it's fun to chew our fruit, too. The recipes in this section make a beautiful presentation—they are healthful candy for the eyes and taste buds. The combination of textures and colors is delightful. Eat these fruit medleys slowly, using a spoon or fork, and savor every bite.

TROPICAL TREES FRUIT SALAD WITH FRUIT SAUCE

Packed with more **vitamin C** than an equivalent amount of orange, the bright green flesh of the kiwifruit, speckled with tiny black seeds, adds a dramatic tropical flair to any fruit salad. Kiwis are a good source of two of the most important fat-soluble antioxidants: **vitamin E** and **vitamin A.** Vitamin A is provided in the form of **beta-carotene.** This combination of both fat-soluble and water-soluble antioxidants allows kiwifruit to provide free radical protection on all fronts.

MAKES 1 BOWL

Fruit Salad:

> **1 kiwifruit, peeled and thinly sliced**
> **¼ cup diced pineapple**
> **2 strawberries, sliced**

To make the fruit salad, combine the kiwifruit, pineapple, and strawberries in a bowl. Toss gently.

Fruit Sauce:

> **1 kiwifruit**
> **½ cup pineapple juice**
> **3 strawberries**
> **1 tablespoon pure maple syrup**

To make the fruit sauce, combine the kiwifruit, pineapple juice, strawberries, and maple syrup in a blender and process until smooth. Pour over the fruit salad and serve.

Mango Banana Fruit Salad...

Mangoes are not only delicious, they are rich in vitamins, minerals, and antioxidants. Mangoes are high in **fiber** but low in calories and sodium; an average-sized mango can contain up to 40 percent of our daily fiber requirement. The deep orange flesh of mangoes is rich in **vitamin A,** with good amounts of **vitamins B** and **C** as well as **potassium, calcium,** and **iron.** Mangoes also contain an **enzyme** with stomach-soothing properties similar to the enzyme papain found in papayas.

MAKES 1 BOWL

Fruit Salad:

> ½ **ripe mango, thinly sliced**
>
> ½ **ripe banana, sliced into rounds**
>
> **4 strawberries, sliced**
>
> **2 pitted dates, thinly sliced**

To make the fruit salad, combine the sliced mango, banana, strawberries, and dates in a bowl. Toss gently.

...WITH FRUIT SAUCE

Fruit Sauce:

> $\frac{1}{2}$ ripe mango
>
> $\frac{1}{2}$ ripe banana
>
> $\frac{1}{2}$ cup papaya or apple juice
>
> $\frac{1}{4}$ cup thinly sliced pitted dates or pure maple syrup
>
> $\frac{1}{4}$ cup ice

Optional Toppings:

> $\frac{1}{3}$ cup raisins
>
> 1 tablespoon coconut flakes
>
> $1\frac{1}{2}$ teaspoons wheat germ

To make the fruit sauce, combine the mango, banana, juice, dates, and ice in a blender and process until smooth. Pour over the fruit salad and top with the optional raisins, coconut flakes, and wheat germ.

GEORGIA PEACH TREAT FRUIT SALAD...

Peaches are easily digested and help stimulate our digestive juices. They have a strong alkaline reaction in the body and can help improve the health of our skin and add color to the complexion. Peaches have mild laxative and diuretic qualities, making them a valuable aid in cleansing the system.

MAKES 1 BOWL

Fruit Salad:

> 1 ripe peach, diced
>
> 1 ripe pear, diced
>
> 1 ripe banana, sliced into rounds

To make the fruit salad, combine the peach, pear, and banana in a bowl. Toss gently.

...WITH FRUIT SAUCE

Fruit Sauce:

> 1 ripe peach
>
> 1 ripe banana
>
> ¼ cup spring water
>
> ¼ cup ice
>
> 1 tablespoon pure maple syrup

Optional Topping:

> 2 tablespoons coconut flakes

To make the fruit sauce, combine the peach, banana, water, ice, and maple syrup in a blender and process until completely smooth. Pour over the fruit salad and top with the optional coconut.

FRUITROPICA SALAD
WITH FRUIT SAUCE

Enjoy this sumptuous combination of sweet peaches, ripe red strawberries, and tropical fruits. It's divine!

MAKES 1 BOWL

Fruit Salad:

> 2 ripe peaches, diced
>
> 1 ripe banana, sliced into rounds
>
> 4 strawberries, sliced
>
> 1/4 cup diced pineapple

For the fruit salad, combine the peaches, banana, strawberries, and pineapple in a bowl. Toss gently.

Fruit Sauce:

> 1 ripe peach
>
> 1 ripe banana
>
> 4 strawberries
>
> 1/4 cup pineapple juice
>
> 1 1/2 teaspoons pure maple syrup

To make the fruit sauce, combine the peach, banana, strawberries, pineapple juice, and maple syrup in a blender and process until smooth. Pour over the fruit salad. Chill and serve.

MANGO-PAPAYA PUDDING

Enjoy this rich-tasting, creamy pudding for breakfast, lunch, dessert, or a snack. The sweet taste is derived solely from the succulent fruits; no added sweetener is needed.

MAKES 1 BOWL

> 1 ripe mango
> 1/2 ripe papaya
> 1/2 ripe banana
> 1/8 teaspoon ground cinnamon

Combine all the ingredients in a blender and process just until smooth. Do not overprocess or the mixture will become too thin. Top with a few slices of the remaining papaya and/or banana, if desired. Eat with a spoon.

FRUIT "UN-PIE"

Indulge your healthy passions with this luscious "ice cream pie." There's no better treat for children or adults.

MAKES 1 BOWL

¼ cup spring water

4 strawberries, sliced

1 tablespoon cranberries

1 tablespoon blueberries

1 tablespoon pure maple syrup

1 cup vanilla soy ice cream

¼ cup granola

Combine the water, strawberries, cranberries, blueberries, and maple syrup in a blender and process until smooth. Pour over the soy ice cream and sprinkle generously with the granola. Eat with a spoon.

GLOSSARY

Acid and Alkali: The pH scale is a ranking of acidity or alkalinity. The "p" stands for potenz, meaning "potential to be," and the "H" is for hydrogen. On this scale, a 7.0 measures neutral—neither acidic nor alkaline. Water is a 7.0. Food with a pH of 6.9 or below is considered an acid; food with a pH of 7.1 or above is considered an alkali or base.

Almond Milk: This delicious, creamy, dairy-free beverage is made by blending blanched almonds with water and straining out the fiber. Almond milk can be made at home; it is also available in aseptic cartons at natural food stores and some supermarkets.

Antioxidant: An antioxidant is any substance that prevents or slows the breakdown of another substance by oxygen. In the body, nutrients such as beta-carotene (a vitamin A precursor), vitamin C, vitamin E, and selenium have been found to perform as antioxidants. They act by scavenging free radicals, which are a normal product of metabolism; the body produces its own antioxidants to keep free radicals in balance. However, stress, aging, and environmental contaminants (such as polluted air and cigarette smoke) can add to the number of free radicals in the body, creating an imbalance. The highly reactive free radicals can damage healthy DNA and have been linked to changes that accompany aging (such as age-related macular degeneration, a leading cause of blindness in older people) and with disease processes that lead to cancer, heart disease, and stroke. Studies have suggested that the antioxidants that occur naturally in fresh fruits and vegetables have a protective effect. For example, vitamin E and beta-carotene appear to protect cell membranes, and vitamin C removes free radicals from inside the cell. Antioxidants in the form of dietary supplements do not appear to counteract the effects of increased numbers of free radicals in the body; in fact, they may actually predispose us to a greater risk of disease. Recent studies indicate that regular consumption of such supplements may interfere with the body's own production of antioxidants. These findings underscore the significance of obtaining our antioxidants directly from fruits and vegetables.

Barley Grass: Barley grass consists of the tender young shoots of the sprouted barley grain. The brilliant green color inherent in barley grass is chlorophyll, the substance that allows plants to photosynthesize. Chlorophyll has the unique ability to break down carbon dioxide and release oxygen; it also has some antibacterial effects. Barley grass is rich in beta-carotene; SOD (superoxide dismutase), a powerful antioxidant; and numerous enzymes, amino acids, vitamins, and minerals. Barley grass is commonly available as a powdered form of green barley juice and can be found in most natural food stores.

Beta-carotene: This is probably the best known of the carotenoids—those red, orange, and yellow pigments that give color to many fruits and vegetables. The body converts beta-carotene into vitamin A, a nutrient that is vital to the growth and development of the human body. As a potent immune-system booster and a powerful antioxidant, beta-carotene counters the effects of cell-damaging molecules called free radicals. Beta-carotene's antioxidant actions make it valuable in protecting against, and in some cases even reversing, certain precancerous conditions. It also may help protect against heart disease, stroke, and cardiovascular disease. Low levels of beta-carotene and other antioxidants have been linked to the development of cataracts, a clouding of the eye's lens that impairs vision. Consuming plenty of fruits and vegetables is an excellent way to supply your body with beta-carotene.

Carob: Native to the eastern Mediterranean, carob is an evergreen tree, *Ceratonia siliqua,* in the pea family; it has feathery leaves and large, dark, leathery pods. The pods contain a sweet, edible pulp and seeds that yield a gum that is used as a stabilizer in food products. The seeds and pods of the carob plant are ground into an edible powder or flour that often is used as a substitute for chocolate or cocoa.

Carob contains high amounts of carbohydrates, calcium, phosphorus, magnesium, silicon, and iron, and it is plentiful in trace minerals. It is a good source of the B vitamins thiamin, riboflavin, and niacin. Carob is approximately 7 percent protein and has a very small amount of fat (in contrast, chocolate is about 50 percent fat). It also is an excellent source of pectin, which makes it a good colon cleanser. Unlike chocolate, carob is nonallergenic and contains no oxalic acid, which interferes with the absorption of calcium. Although its taste is not quite the same as chocolate, carob imparts a rich, dark flavor that makes it a good chocolate alternative in beverages and baked goods.

Cayenne: Cayenne is a member of the *Capsicum* family, more commonly known as chili peppers. The hotness produced by cayenne is caused by its high concentration of a substance called capsaicin, which has been widely studied for its pain-reducing effects, cardiovascular benefits, and ability to help prevent ulcers. The peppery heat of capsaicin also effectively opens and drains congested nasal passages.

Cayenne and other red chili peppers have been shown to reduce blood cholesterol, triglyceride levels, and platelet aggregation, while increasing the body's ability to dissolve fibrin, a substance integral to the formation of blood clots. In addition to its high capsaicin content, cayenne's bright red color signals its abundance of beta-carotene (provitamin A), one of the most important antioxidants in the body.

Chlorophyll: This green pigment in plants is essential to the photosynthesis reactions that convert radiant energy from the sun into chemical energy for life processes. Inside the cells of green plants, chlorophyll combines with carbon dioxide and sunlight to form simple sugars. Without chlorophyll, plants would be unable to perform essential metabolic functions, such as respiration and growth.

Due to its natural deodorizing ability, chlorophyll has traditionally been used as a mouthwash and gargle. Chlorophyll has been shown to stimulate liver function and the excretion of bile, strengthen immunity, and detoxify chemical pollutants. Recent studies show promise that chlorophyll may also have anticarcinogenic and antimutagenic properties. Chlorophyll is found in the highest concentrations in green leafy vegetables, such as spinach and kale, and in cereal grasses, such as wheat grass and barley grass.

Coconut Milk: Coconuts are the drupaceous fruit of the coconut palm, whose outer fibrous husk yields a thick, course fiber and whose nut contains a dense, edible meat. The liquid inside coconuts is called "coconut water"; it is very sweet and clear with a slight cream-colored tint. You can drink this liquid as a beverage or add it to cereal or shakes.

Coconut milk is made by soaking the grated flesh of a coconut in hot water, then straining it. Coconut milk is classified as thick, thin, or coconut cream. Thick coconut milk is the result of the first soaking and squeezing. If this milk is refrigerated it separates, and the top layer is the cream. Thin coconut milk is what is produced when the coconut meat is soaked and strained a second time. Canned coconut milk separates naturally, so shake the can well before using.

Dehydration: Dehydration means your body does not have as much water and fluids as it should. Dehydration can be caused by losing too much fluid, not drinking enough water or other fluids, or both. Infants and children are more susceptible to dehydration than adults because of their smaller body weights and higher turnover of water and electrolytes. The elderly and those with illnesses are also at higher risk. Dehydration is classified as mild, moderate, or severe based on how much of the body's fluid is lost or not replenished. When severe, dehydration is a life-threatening emergency.

Enzymes: The human body is capable of producing over twenty-two digestive enzymes, which are biological catalysts that help us digest protein, carbohydrates, sugars, and fats. The process of digestion begins in the mouth (with chewing and the production of saliva) and continues throughout the digestive system, where various enzymes go to work breaking down the foods we eat. Enzymes found in plant foods enhance the efficiency of our digestion.

Ginger: Native to southeastern Asia, this aromatic, pungent seasoning is the thick, underground rhizome of the ginger plant, known botanically as *Zingiber officinale*. Fresh gingerroot is available year-round in the produce section of your local market. The flesh of the gingerroot may be yellow, white, or red, depending on the variety. It is covered with a papery, brownish skin that may be thick or thin, depending on whether the plant was mature or young when it was harvested. Powdered ginger, made from the ground dried root, is available in the spice aisle of most supermarkets.

Ginger has a long tradition of being very effective in alleviating the symptoms of gastrointestinal distress. It is regarded as an excellent carminative (a substance that promotes the elimination of intestinal gas) and intestinal spasmolytic (a substance that relaxes and soothes the intestinal tract). Ginger reduces all the symptoms related to motion sickness, including dizziness, nausea, vomiting, and cold sweating, and has been shown to be very useful in reducing the nausea and vomiting associated with pregnancy.

Ginger contains very potent anti-inflammatory compounds called gingerols. This may explain why ginger, when consumed regularly, has been useful in reducing pain levels and improving mobility in people with osteoarthritis and rheumatoid arthritis.

Whenever possible, choose fresh ginger over the dried form, since fresh gingerroot is not only superior in flavor, it contains higher levels of gingerol. Ginger is so concentrated with active substances that you don't have to use very much to receive its beneficial effects.

Granola: This crunchy cereal mix is typically a combination of rolled oats, dried fruits, nuts, and honey or brown sugar. It is a good source of fiber and protein, and makes a tasty and substantial breakfast food or snack.

Immunity: The immune system consists of cells, cell products, organs, and structures of the body involved in the detection and destruction of foreign invaders, such as bacteria, viruses, and cancer cells.

Immunity is based on our system's ability to resist or launch a defense against such invaders.

Kelp: Sea vegetables, especially kelp, are among nature's richest sources of iodine. They are also abundant in folic acid and are a very good source of magnesium, both of which can help reduce high blood pressure and prevent heart attacks. Sea vegetables can support our bodies during periods of high stress by supplying not only magnesium but pantothenic acid and riboflavin—two B vitamins necessary for energy production.

Kelp and other sea vegetables are also good sources of iron and calcium. In addition, sea vegetables contain good amounts of lignans, plant compounds with promising anticancer properties. Kelp is light brown to dark green in color; it is available in flakes or powdered form at natural food stores.

Molasses: This thick, dark syrup is produced by boiling down the juice from sugar cane during the process of sugar refining. It is rich in several minerals, including calcium and iron.

Nut Butters: The most famous nut butter is peanut butter, a spread made from roasted peanuts, which are actually a legume, not a tree nut. Peanuts are a good source of protein as well as vitamin E, niacin, folate, and magnesium. They also are rich in heart-healthy monounsaturated fat and are an excellent source of biotin, a B vitamin involved in the metabolism of both sugar and fat. Luscious spreads made from various tree nuts and seeds are readily available, with the greatest variety found at natural food stores. These include almond butter, cashew butter, sesame tahini, and pumpkin seed butter, among many others. While each nut or seed butter has its own special characteristics, they all are rich sources of healthy fats, protein, and a variety of important vitamins and minerals.

Rice Milk: Rice milk is made from cooked rice that is blended with water and strained. It is a bit sweeter and not as creamy or rich tasting as soymilk, and it is lower in both protein and fat. Rice milk is readily available in aseptic cartons at natural food stores. It comes plain or flavored. Rice milk is a good hypoallergenic alternative to soymilk and almond milk.

Soymilk: This creamy nondairy beverage is made by soaking soybeans, grinding them with water, and straining out the solids. You can make soymilk at home with basic kitchen tools or with a special soymilk machine. Soymilk is also sold in natural food stores and many major supermarkets. It is commonly packaged in aseptic cartons, which keep it shelf stable for many months if unopened; fresh soymilk can be found in the dairy case. Soymilk is available plain, sweetened, or flavored, and most brands are fortified with calcium, vitamins D and B_{12}, and sometimes other nutrients.

Vegan: A person who abstains from consuming and using animal products and their derivatives is called vegan. Food, clothing, and other items that are free of animal products are also referred to as vegan.

Vegetarian Protein Powder: Protein is the nitrogenous material of living matter (plant or animal) and is essential for tissue repair and growth. The protein powder recommended for the recipes in this book is made from pure plant proteins and contains no animal products or by-products. It also should contain no dairy products or dairy derivatives, such as milk, whey, or casein. Please read product labels and ingredient lists thoroughly before purchasing your protein powder. Usually there is a toll-free number on the back of the package for consumers to call with questions about the product and any of its ingredients.

INDEX

A

acidifying foods 15
acidity 85
actinidin 72
alfalfa sprouts
    Vegetable Combo Four 41
alkalinity 85
alkalizing foods 16
almond butter 90
almond milk, about 85
    Banana Moon 75
    Cranberry Crunch 62–63
    Eternity Winter 52
    Fruity Ice Cream Soy Shake 39
    Hazelnut Heaven 58
    Protein Shake 59
    Second Resurrection 48
almonds
    Coconut Date Shake 38
antioxidants 20, 34, 49, 52, 68, 72, 85–86
apple juice
    Mango Banana Fruit Salad 78–79
apples, about 34
    Quick-Me-Up 34

B

bananas, about 33, 34, 48, 68, 75
    Banana Breeze 68
    Banana Moon 75
    Everlasting Life 33
    Fruitropica 82
    Georgia Peach Treat Fruit Salad 80–81
    Hazelnut Heaven 58
    Mango Banana Fruit Salad 78–79
    Mango-Papaya Pudding 83
    Oat Breakfast Shake 69
    Protein Shake 59
    Quick-Me-Up 34
    Second Resurrection 48
    Tropical Dream 74
barley grass 86
barley juice
    Vegetable Combo Four 41
barley malt 11

bee pollen, about 45
    Vegetable Combo Five 45
beets, about 45
    Vegetable Combo Five 45
beta-carotene in various foods 31, 41, 48, 53, 60, 77, 85, 86, 87
betacyanin 45
bioflavonoids 27
biotin 90
blenders and other equipment 17
blueberries
    Fruit "Un-Pie" 84
    Fruity Ice Cream Soy Shake 39
    Very Berry Fine 65
breakfast, menu recommendations for 10
bromelain 44

C

caffeic acid 49
calcium in various foods 22, 36, 41, 66, 78, 90, 91
capsaicin 87
carob 13, 86–87
    Eternity Winter 52
    The Resurrection 35
carotenes 65
carotenoids 31, 60
carrots, about 31, 41, 66
    Vegetable Combos 22–23, 31, 36, 41, 45, 66
cashew butter 90
cashews
    Coconut Date Shake 38
catechins 52, 72
cayenne 87
    Purification 24
centrifugal juicers 17
chlorophyll 33, 41, 87–88
chocolate 13, 86–87
choline 53
cocoa 13, 86
coconut milk, about 88
    Banana Breeze 68
    Coconut Date Shake 38
    Pineapple Supreme Piña Colada 44
    Tropical Dream 74
collagen 65
copper in various foods 36, 58, 69
corn syrup 12
cranberries, about 62
    Cranberry Crunch 62–63
    Fruit "Un-Pie" 84
    Very Berry Fine 65

cucumbers, about 49, 50
    Cucumber Lemonade 49
    Vegetable Combos 50, 60, 66

D

dairy products 13–14
dandelion 22–23
dates 11
    Coconut Date Shake 38
    Mango Banana Fruit Salad 78–79
dehydration 88
    Rehydration Drink 64
detoxification 26–27
dextrose 12
digestive problems 14
dinner, menu recommendations for 10
diuretics 27, 50

E

echinacea 31
enzymes 88
Eternity Winter 52
Everlasting Life 33

F

fats, in nut butters 90
fats, monounsaturated 58
fiber in various foods 36, 58, 65, 69, 75, 78
fibrin 87
filtered pressing 17
flavonoids 52, 65, 72
folate in various foods 22, 58, 60, 65, 69, 90
folic acid 33, 66, 90
food combining 15–16
free radicals 85, 86
Fresh Freeze 71
Fresh Quench 29
Fruitropica 82
fruit salads
    Fruitropica 82
    Georgia Peach Treat 80–81
    Mango Banana 78–79
    Tropical Trees 77
fruit sauces 77, 79, 81, 82
Fruit "Un-Pie" 84
fruit, using as a sweetener 11

G

Georgia Peach Treat Fruit Salad 80–81
Ginger Get Well 30
gingerroot, about 89
    Ginger Get Well 30
    Vegetable Combo Two 31
granola, about 89
    Cranberry Crunch 62–63
    Fruit "Un-Pie" 84

Grape Drink, Daily 27
grapefruit, about 29
    Detoxification 26
    Fresh Quench 29
graters 17
greens, about 66
    Vegetable Combos 36, 66
grinders 17

H

hazelnuts, about 58
    Hazelnut Heaven 58
Hebrew Sunrise 53
high-fructose corn syrup 12
honey 11–12

I

ice cream, soy or nondairy
    Banana Moon 75
    Fruit "Un-Pie" 84
    Fruity Ice Cream Soy Shake 39
    The Resurrection 35
immune strengthening 30
immunity 89–90
iodine 33, 90
iron in various foods 22, 33, 36, 38, 41, 66,
    78, 90

J

juicers 17
juices, hints for making 13–14

K

kale, about 36
    Vegetable Combos 36, 66
kelp 90
kelp powder
    Everlasting Life 33
    Last Man Standing 43
    Rehydration Drink 64
    Vegetable Combo Three 36
kiwi, about 72, 77
    Kiwi Lemonade 72
    Tropical Cooler 56
    Tropical Trees Fruit Salad 77

L

Last Man Standing 43
lecithin 53
lemons, about 24, 55, 72
    Cucumber Lemonade 49
    Detoxification 26
    Fresh Quench 29
    Kiwi Lemonade 72
    Lemonade 55
    Purification 24
    Rehydration Drink 64
    Vegetable Combos 22–23, 60

lettuce
Vegetable Combo Five 45
lignans 90
lunch, menu recommendations for 10
lutein 60
lycopene 20

M
magnesium in various foods 41, 49, 58, 60,
65, 66, 89
manganese in various foods 36, 60, 66, 69
mangoes, about 53
Fruity Ice Cream Soy Shake 39
Hebrew Sunrise 53
Mango Banana Fruit Salad 78–79
Mango Melody 40
Mango-Papaya Pudding 83
maple syrup 12
milk, nondairy
Banana Breeze 68
Banana Moon 75
Coconut Date Shake 38
Cranberry Crunch 62–63
Eternity Winter 52
Fruity Ice Cream Soy Shake 39
Hazelnut Heaven 58
Protein Shake 59
Quick-Me-Up 34
Second Resurrection 48
The Resurrection 35
molasses 90
monounsaturated fats 58
mucilages 22

N
niacin 90
nucleic acids 48
nut butters 90
nutritional recommendations 9
nuts, soaking 13

O
oats, about 59, 69
Oat Breakfast Shake 69
oat straw 59
omega-3 fatty acids 66
oranges
Detoxification 26
Fresh Quench 29
Hebrew Sunrise 53
Mango Melody 40
Pineapple Supreme Piña Colada 44

P
pantothenic acid 65, 66, 90

papain 65, 72, 78
papaya, about 65
Mango Pudding 83
papaya juice
Mango Banana Fruit Salad 78–79
Very Berry Fine 65
peaches, about 80
Fruitropica 82
Georgia Peach Treat Fruit Salad 80–81
Mango Melody 40
Peach Deliverance 47
peanut butter 90
pears
Georgia Peach Treat Fruit Salad 80–81
pectin 87
pH scale 85
phosphatidylcholine 53
phosphorus 58, 66, 69
phytochemicals 40, 65
Pie, Fruit "Un-" 84
pineapple, about 44
Banana Breeze 68
Fresh Freeze 71
Fruitropica 82
Fruity Ice Cream Soy Shake 39
Ginger Get Well 30
Pineapple Supreme Piña Colada 44
Tropical Cooler 56
Tropical Trees Fruit Salad 77
pineapple juice
Fresh Freeze 71
Fruitropica 82
Hebrew Sunrise 53
Peach Deliverance 47
Tropical Cooler 56
Tropical Dream 74
Tropical Trees Fruit Salad 77
potassium in various foods 22, 33, 41, 49,
58, 62, 65, 66, 75, 78
proanthocyanidins 62
protein powder, vegetarian, about 91
Everlasting Life 33
Last Man Standing 43
Protein Shake 59
Quick-Me-Up 34
Pudding, Mango-Papaya 83
pumpkin seed butter 90
pumpkin seeds
Last Man Standing 43
Purification 24

Q
quercetin 34, 60

R

reamers 17
Rehydration Drink 64
Resurrection 35
riboflavin 66, 90
rice milk, about 90–91
    Cranberry Crunch 62–63
    Fruity Ice Cream Soy Shake 39
    Quick-Me-Up 34
    Second Resurrection 48

S

sea vegetables 90
seeds, soaking 13
selenium 58, 69, 85
sesame seeds
    Last Man Standing 43
sesame tahini 33, 90
shakes
    Coconut Date 38
    Fruity Soy Ice Cream 39
    Oat Breakfast 69
    Protein 59
silica 49, 59
soy ice cream
    Banana Moon 75
    Fruit "Un-Pie" 84
    Fruity Ice Cream Soy Shake 39
    The Resurrection 35
soymilk, about 91
    Banana Breeze 68
    Banana Moon 75
    Coconut Date Shake 38
    Cranberry Crunch 62–63
    Fruity Ice Cream Soy Shake 39
    Quick-Me-Up 34
    Second Resurrection 48
    The Resurrection 35
spinach, about 60
    Vegetable Combos 41, 60
spirulina 33
spirulina powder 31, 35, 36
    Last Man Standing 43
    Second Resurrection 48
    The Resurrection 35
    Vegetable Combos 36, 60, 66
sterols, plant 58
stevia 12
strawberries, about 34
    Banana Breeze 68
    Fresh Freeze 71
    Fruit "Un-Pie" 84

strawberries, about (continued)
    Fruitropica 82
    Mango Banana Fruit Salad 78–79
    Oat Breakfast Shake 69
    Quick-Me-Up 34
    Tropical Cooler 56
    Tropical Dream 74
    Tropical Trees Fruit Salad 77
    Very Berry Fine 65
sweeteners 11–12

T

tahini 33, 90
thiamin 69
trituration 17
Tropical Cooler 56
Tropical Dream 74
Tropical Trees Fruit Salad 77

V

veganism 91
vegetable combos
    One 22–23
    Two 31
    Three 36
    Four 41
    Five 45
    Six 50
    Seven 60
    Eight 66
Very Berry Fine 65
vitamin A in various foods 90, 22, 31, 36, 41, 62, 66, 77, 78, 85
vitamin B (complex) 66, 87
vitamin B_1 36
vitamin B_2 36
vitamin B_6 34, 36, 53
vitamin B_{12} 62, 91
vitamin C in various foods 20, 22, 24, 34, 36, 41, 44, 47, 49, 53, 62, 65, 66, 72, 77, 78, 85
vitamin D 91
vitamin E in various foods 33, 36, 53, 58, 69, 77, 85, 90
vitamin K 60, 72
vitamin P 27

W

walnuts
    Coconut Date Shake 38
Watermelon Juice 20–21

Z

zinc 43, 58, 69

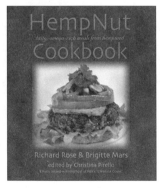